Your hard work and dedicati

Thanks for all yc...

EMP

Emergency Medicine Physicians

The **Best** in Emergency Medicine

COMMITMENT TO EXCELLENCE™

Celebrating the Very Best

Compiled by Kobi Yamada
Designed by Steve Potter and Jenica Wilkie

COM·PEN´·DI·UM™
Publishing

*E*nriching the lives of millions, one person at a time.™

ACKNOWLEDGEMENTS

These quotations were gathered lovingly but unscientifically over several years and/or contributed by many friends or acquaintances. Some arrived—and survived in our files—on scraps of paper and may therefore be imperfectly worded or attributed. To the authors, contributors and original sources, our thanks, and where appropriate, our apologies. —The editors

WITH SPECIAL THANKS TO

Jason Aldrich, Gerry Baird, Jay Baird, Justi Baumgardt, Neil Beaton, Rob & Beth Bingham, Doug Cruickshank, Jim Darragh, Kari Cassidy-Diercks, Kyle Diercks, Josie and Rob Estes, Jennifer Hurwitz, Dick Kamm, Beth Keane, Liam Lavery, Connie McMartin, Jim & Teri O'Brien, Janet Potter & Family, Diane Roger, Cristal Spurr, Sam Sundquist, Jenica Wilkie, Heidi Wills, Robert & Val Yamada, Tote Yamada, Anne Zadra, and August & Arline Zadra

CREDITS

Compiled by Kobi Yamada
Designed by Steve Potter and Jenica Wilkie

ISBN: 1-932319-02-6

Printed in Hong Kong

CONTENTS

CELEBRATING THE VERY BEST

*A first-rate soup is more creative
than a second-rate painting.*

—Abraham Maslow

Down deep inside no one really wants to be average. Average is that vast nowhere land in the middle of the pack. Average is the best of the worst, or the worst of the best—and who really wants to live and work in a place like that?

"Starting today," wrote Tom Peters, "let's banish the philosophy of mediocrity. No matter what your occupation or endeavor, excellence is what you and your people create on your turf. It can be done and it is done. There is no excuse for not getting on with it among your people."

COMMITMENT TO

The truth is, no calling on earth is insignificant if it is accomplished with pride and artistry. Examples are everywhere. When Ray Kroc founded McDonald's he proclaimed, "the french fry is my canvas." Another example: at Dunkin Donuts a 23-page specification proudly lists the requirements for a quality cup of coffee. Coffee must be brewed at precisely 197 degrees and served within 18 minutes to qualify as a Dunkin Donuts "masterpiece." If 5,000 Dunkin Donuts franchises are committed to excellence, why aren't we?

The good news is that whoever you are and whatever you are doing, some kind of excellence is within your reach. Just give the very best you have to the highest you know. Do something brilliant every day. Make a great meal tonight. Sell something in a dynamic way. Spectacularly deliver a presentation. Tell an outstanding joke. Slash through a difficult obstacle. Dream a wonderful dream.

E X C E L L E N C E

COMMITMENT TO

Most of us never qualify

for life's grand awards; no

Oscar, Emmy or Nobel Prize.

But we all have a shot at

one worthwhile pursuit—the

chance to deliver quality in

Q U A L I T Y

all that we do for others.

Quality comes from the head,

the hands, and the heart; it

is never an accident, always

an intention. Take good and

make it great. Take great

and make it best.

QUALITY IS NOT ANY SINGLE THING BUT
AN AURA, AN ATMOSPHERE, AN OVER-
POWERING FEELING THAT A COMPANY IS
DOING EVERYTHING WITH EXCELLENCE.

—Jack Welch

NO MATTER WHAT BUSINESS WE'RE IN,
THE GOAL IS QUALITY AND THE
CHALLENGE IS REACHING IT.

—Fred Smith

ONLY PEOPLE CAN SUPPLY QUALITY.

—Philip B. Crosby

C O M M I T M E N T

THE REAL ISSUE IS VALUE, NOT PRICE.

—Robert T. Lindgren

HALF OF SUCCESS IS THINKING THAT WHAT WE ARE DOING HAS GOT TO BE DONE THE BEST ANYBODY EVER DID IT.

—Helen Gurley Brown

QUALITY IS A PROUD AND SOARING THING.

—Jessica Julian

9

T O   Q U A L I T Y

THE REAL SECRET OF JOY IN WORK IS
CONTAINED IN ONE WORD—EXCELLENCE.
TO KNOW HOW TO DO SOMETHING WELL
IS TO ENJOY IT.

—Pearl Buck

10

WHEN YOU LOVE YOUR WORK,
IT SHOWS.

—Audrey Woodhall

ONE OF THE GREATEST SOURCES
OF ENERGY IS PRIDE IN WHAT YOU
ARE DOING.

—Don Ward

C O M M I T M E N T

QUALITY IS NOT JUST A CHART, OR A
STANDARD, OR A SPECIFICATION—IT'S
A STATE OF MIND, A COMMITMENT,
A RESPONSIBILITY, A SPIRIT. IT'S
A WAY OF DOING, BEING AND LIVING.

—Don Galer

HOLD YOURSELF TO A HIGHER STANDARD
THAN ANYBODY ELSE EXPECTS OF YOU.

—Henry Ward Beecher

BE FANATICS. WHEN IT COMES TO
BEING, DOING AND DREAMING THE BEST,
BE MANIACS.

—A.M. Rosenthal

T O   Q U A L I T Y

GOOD IS NOT GOOD WHERE BETTER IS
EXPECTED.

—Thomas Fuller

IT'S A FUNNY THING ABOUT LIFE. IF WE
REFUSE TO ACCEPT ANYTHING BUT THE
VERY BEST, WE VERY OFTEN GET IT.

—Somerset Maugham

I AM EASILY SATISFIED WITH THE
VERY BEST.

—Winston Churchill

COMMITMENT

WHEN WE BUILD, LET US THINK THAT WE
BUILD FOREVER.

—John Ruskin

IN COMMUNITIES WHERE MEN BUILD SHIPS
FOR THEIR OWN SONS TO FISH OR FIGHT
FROM, QUALITY IS NEVER A PROBLEM.

13

—J. Deville

QUALITY BEGINS WITH CHARACTER.

—Amos Laurence

T O   Q U A L I T Y

QUALITY IS NOT A PROGRAM, IT'S A WAY OF LIFE.

—Charles "Chic" Thompson

THERE IS NO SUCH THING AS A MINOR LAPSE OF INTEGRITY.

—Tom Peters

14

INTEGRITY IS NOT NEGOTIABLE.

—Pat "PK" Koran

C O M M I T M E N T

IF YOU WALK BY A PROBLEM, NO MATTER
HOW LITTLE IT IS, YOU AS A LEADER HAVE
SET A NEW STANDARD.

—Wayne Downing

INTEGRITY IS NOT A SOMETIME THING,
IT'S AN ALL THE TIME THING.

—Peter Sotese

THERE IS ABSOLUTELY NO REASON FOR
HAVING ERRORS OR DEFECTS IN ANY
PRODUCT.

—Philip B. Crosby

T   O   Q   U   A   L   I   T   Y

WHEN A COMPANY COMPROMISES ITS PRINCIPLES ONE TIME, THE NEXT COMPROMISE IS RIGHT AROUND THE CORNER.

—Zig Ziglar

NEVER SURRENDER YOURSELF TO THE MOMENTUM OF MEDIOCRITY.

—Justi Baumgardt

MEDIOCRITY IS THE ENEMY.

—Don Galer

C O M M I T M E N T

AS YOU MOVE FORWARD, CHECK EACH STEP FOR ERROR. IF YOU DON'T CATCH IT, YOU INHERIT IT.

—Don Ward

DOING YOUR BEST AT THIS MOMENT PUTS YOU IN THE BEST PLACE FOR THE NEXT MOMENT.

—Oprah Winfrey

DO IT RIGHT THE FIRST TIME. DO IT VERY RIGHT THE SECOND TIME.

—Steven Marciani

T O   Q U A L I T Y

DON'T BE AFRAID TO GIVE UP THE GOOD
TO GO FOR THE GREAT.

—Kenny Rogers

EVERY DAY IS AN OPPORTUNITY TO
CHANGE THINGS FOR THE BETTER.

—Michael Pivec

GOOD, BETTER, BEST; NEVER LET IT
REST,'TIL YOUR GOOD IS BETTER, AND
YOUR BETTER BEST.

—Early American children's rhyme

COMMITMENT

IF THINGS WERE DONE RIGHT ONLY 99.9%
OF THE TIME, WE'D HAVE TWO UNSAFE
PLANE LANDINGS PER DAY AT O'HARE AND
16,000 LOST PIECES OF MAIL EVERY HOUR
BY THE U.S. POSTAL SERVICE. STRIVE FOR
100% QUALITY!

—*Jeff Dewar*

IF YOU HAVEN'T GOT THE TIME TO DO IT
RIGHT, WHEN WILL YOU FIND THE TIME TO
DO IT OVER?

—*Jeffery J. Mayer*

PAY ATTENTION TO THOSE DETAILS.
SWEAT THE SMALL STUFF.

—*United Technologies*

T O Q U A L I T Y

THERE ARE NO SHORTCUTS TO ANY PLACE
WORTH GOING.

—*Beverly Sills*

DISCIPLINE IS THE WHOLE KEY TO BEING
SUCCESSFUL. WE ALL GET 24 HOURS A
DAY. IT'S THE ONLY FAIR THING; IT'S THE
ONLY THING THAT'S EQUAL. IT'S UP TO
US AS TO WHAT WE DO WITH THOSE 24
HOURS.

—*Sam Huff*

BE A YARDSTICK OF QUALITY. SOME
PEOPLE AREN'T USED TO AN ENVIRONMENT
WHERE EXCELLENCE IS EXPECTED.

—*Steven Jobs*

COMMITMENT

FIX YOUR EYES ON PERFECTION AND YOU CAN MAKE ALMOST EVERYTHING SPEED TOWARDS IT.

—W.E. Cummings

PEOPLE NEVER IMPROVE UNLESS THEY LOOK TO SOME STANDARD OR EXAMPLE HIGHER OR BETTER THAN THEMSELVES.

—Tryon Edwards

OF ALL HUMAN RESOURCES, THE MOST PRECIOUS IS THE DESIRE TO IMPROVE.

—Susan Fielder

T O Q U A L I T Y

WE DON'T REMAIN GOOD IF WE DON'T
ALWAYS STRIVE TO BECOME BETTER.
—Gottfried Keller

PRACTICE YOURSELF IN LITTLE THINGS,
THENCE PROCEED TO GREATER.
—Epictetus

GOOD ENOUGH IS NEVER GOOD ENOUGH.
—Sharon Banta

COMMITMENT

SCHOOL IS NEVER OUT FOR THE PRO.

—*Jim Williamson*

I THINK THE ONE LESSON I HAVE
LEARNED IS THAT THERE IS NO
SUBSTITUTE FOR PAYING ATTENTION.

—*Diane Sawyer*

WHATEVER YOU ARE, BE A GOOD ONE.

—*Abraham Lincoln*

TO QUALITY

CARING IS THE ULTIMATE COMPETITIVE
ADVANTAGE.

—Ron Kendrick

CUSTOMERS CAN SMELL EMOTIONAL
COMMITMENT A MILE AWAY. EVERY
SINGLE PERSON IN THE ENTIRE ORGANIZA-
TION NEEDS TO SPEAK THE LANGUAGE OF
QUALITY VERY FLUENTLY.

—Tom Peters

QUALITY IN A PRODUCT OR SERVICE IS NOT
DETERMINED BY WHAT YOU PUT INTO IT,
BUT BY WHAT THE CLIENT OR CUSTOMER
GETS OUT OF IT.

—Paul Toth

COMMITMENT

THE QUALITY OF ANY PRODUCT OR SERVICE IS WHAT THE CUSTOMER SAYS IT IS.

—Techsonic

TO SUCCEED, TRY TO SEE HOW MUCH YOU CAN GIVE FOR A DOLLAR, INSTEAD OF HOW LITTLE YOU CAN GIVE FOR A DOLLAR.

—Henry Ford

WHEN IT COMES TO YOUR PRODUCT OR PROJECT, PEOPLE WILL TAKE QUALITY AS SERIOUSLY AS YOU DO—NO MORE SO.

—Philip B. Crosby

T O   Q U A L I T Y

TECHNIQUES DON'T PRODUCE QUALITY
PRODUCTS; PEOPLE DO, PEOPLE WHO CARE,
PEOPLE WHO ARE TREATED AS CREATIVELY
CONTRIBUTING ADULTS.

—Tom Peters

26 PLEASURE IN THE JOB PUTS PERFECTION
IN THE WORK.

—Aristotle

OUR PEOPLE ARE RESPONSIBLE FOR
THEIR OWN PRODUCT AND ITS QUALITY.
WE EXPECT THEM TO ACT LIKE OWNERS.

—Gordon Forward

COMMITMENT

IT IS NOT WHO IS RIGHT, BUT WHAT IS
RIGHT, THAT'S IMPORTANT.

—Thomas Huxley

THERE ARE NO LITTLE THINGS.
"LITTLE THINGS" ARE THE THINGS OF
THE UNIVERSE.

—Fanny Fern

BY THE WORK ONE KNOWS THE WORKMAN.

—Jean De La Fontaine

T   O   Q   U   A   L   I   T   Y

WHEN HEART AND SKILL WORK TOGETHER,
EXPECT A MASTERPIECE.

—C. Reade

PERFECTION IS FINALLY ATTAINED, NOT
WHEN THERE IS NO LONGER ANYTHING
TO ADD, BUT WHEN THERE IS NO LONGER
ANYTHING TO TAKE AWAY.

—Antoine De Saint-Exupery

LIFE'S TWO CHIEF PRIZES, BEAUTY
AND TRUTH, I FOUND THE FIRST IN
A LOVING HEART AND THE SECOND
IN A LABORER'S HAND.

—Kahlil Gibran

COMMITMENT

NOBODY WHO EVER GAVE HIS BEST
REGRETTED IT.

—George Halas

IF YOU BELIEVE IN UNLIMITED QUALITY
AND ACT IN ALL YOUR BUSINESS
DEALINGS WITH TOTAL INTEGRITY,
THE REST WILL TAKE CARE OF ITSELF.

—Frank Perdue

WE LOVE QUALITY.

—Robert Campeau

29

TO QUALITY

COMMITMENT TO

Service is not a set of rules or off-the-shelf solutions, it is a constant process of discovery. To be of real service, one must be willing to discover exactly what the other person wants

S E R V I C E

or needs—and then provide it. "In business, as in life," wrote Malcolm Dowling, "we all take turns serving each other. Let there be energy and pride at every turn."

SERVICE ISN'T A BIG THING.
IT'S A MILLION LITTLE THINGS.

—Unknown

ALL OF US ARE THE COMPANY, AND EACH
OF US MUST BE COMMITTED TO PROVIDING
SUPERIOR VALUE AND PERSONALIZED
SERVICE EVERY SINGLE TIME TO OUR
CUSTOMERS.

—Frank Vizzare

YOU NEVER GET A SECOND CHANCE
TO MAKE A FIRST IMPRESSION!

—J.H. Bockley

COMMITMENT

THE ESSENTIAL DIFFERENCE IN SERVICE
IS NOT MACHINES OR THINGS. THE
ESSENTIAL DIFFERENCE IS MINDS,
HEARTS, SPIRITS AND SOULS.

—Herb Kelleher

YOUR WORK IS A MIRROR IMAGE OF
YOURSELF AND THE COMPANY YOU WORK
FOR. WHAT SHOWS ON THE OUTSIDE IS
A GOOD INDICATION OF WHAT IS TAKING
PLACE ON THE INSIDE.

—Charlotte Elich

ALL OTHER THINGS BEING EQUAL,
CUSTOMERS WILL GO WHERE THEY
CONTINUOUSLY FEEL MASSIVELY
LIKED OR LOVED.

—Jim Cecil

TO SERVICE

CUSTOMERS ARE NOT DEPENDENT ON US,
WE ARE DEPENDENT ON THEM.

—Faye Holliday

OUR CHECKS THAT GO TO OUR PEOPLE SAY,
'FROM OUR CUSTOMERS,' BECAUSE WE
WANT TO REMIND OURSELVES THAT IT'S
NOT SOME ADDITION TO THE GENERAL
OFFICE THAT PRODUCES THAT CHECK;
IT'S OUR CUSTOMERS.

—Herb Kelleher

ONE OF THE MOST IMPORTANT LESSONS OF
BUSINESS — THE VALUE OF CONCENTRATING
ON THE CUSTOMERS YOU HAVE.

—Tom Monaghan

COMMITMENT

OUR CUSTOMERS WILL BEGIN TO REALIZE
THAT THEY REALLY CAN COUNT ON FASTER,
CRISPER, MORE CARING AND PERSONAL
SERVICE FROM US. THAT SPECIAL
RELATIONSHIP TRANSLATES INTO REAL
VALUE FOR OUR CUSTOMERS—AND WHEN
OUR CUSTOMERS WIN, WE WIN.

—Ron Kendrick

EVERY ROUTINE EYE-TO-EYE CONTACT
WITH THE CUSTOMER IS A MOMENT OF
TRUTH. IT'S A GOLDEN OPPORTUNITY
FOR EACH EMPLOYEE TO PERSONALLY
DEMONSTRATE THE UNIQUE SPIRIT AND
SERVICE OF THE COMPANY.

—Don Ward

T O   S E R V I C E

WHEN CUSTOMERS LEAVE US FOR GREENER PASTURES, THEY USUALLY GIVE PRICE AS THE REASON, WHEN IN FACT IT'S SIMPLE NEGLECT.

—John R. Graham

INSTEAD OF "I DON'T KNOW," SAY "I'LL FIND OUT." INSTEAD OF "YOU'LL HAVE TO," SAY, "HERE'S HOW I CAN HELP YOU." INSTEAD OF "HANG ON FOR A SECOND," SAY, "ARE YOU ABLE TO HOLD FOR A MINUTE WHILE I CHECK?" INSTEAD OF, "WE CAN'T DO THAT," SAY, "THAT'S A TOUGH ONE, BUT LET'S SEE WHAT WE CAN DO."

—Jim Williamson

COMPANIES, GREAT AND SMALL, DO RISE AND FALL ONE CUSTOMER AT A TIME.

—Dan Zadra

COMMITMENT

ANY BENEFIT A CUSTOMER CAN'T
UNDERSTAND DOESN'T EXIST.

—Jan Carlzon

THE FIRST TIME YOU SAY," THE
CUSTOMER IS STUPID," WRITE DOWN
THE DATE AND TIME; BECAUSE THE DAY
WILL COME WHEN YOU WILL WANT TO
KNOW THE EXACT MOMENT YOUR
BUSINESS BEGAN TO DECLINE.

—Stephen G. Largy

TREAT ALL PEOPLE WITH DIGNITY
AND RESPECT.

—John Wooden

T O   S E R V I C E

IT TAKES 20 YEARS TO BUILD A
REPUTATION AND FIVE MINUTES TO RUIN
IT. IF YOU THINK ABOUT THAT, YOU'LL
DO THINGS DIFFERENTLY.

—Warren Buffet

IT'S NOT WHAT WE DO NOW AND THEN
THAT COUNTS—IT'S WHAT WE DO EVERY
DAY, EVERY TIME, AND WITH EVERY
SINGLE CUSTOMER THAT REALLY COUNTS.

—Ron Kendrick

AS LONG AS THE DAY LASTS,
LET'S GIVE IT ALL WE'VE GOT.

—David O. McKay

COMMITMENT

AS A CORPORATION GETS BIGGER AND
BIGGER YOU NEED TO DO EVERYTHING
POSSIBLE TO MAKE IT SEEM SMALLER
AND SMALLER.

—Craig Barrett

ACT AS IF WHAT YOU DO MAKES A
DIFFERENCE. IT DOES.

—William James

AS AN ORGANIZATION GROWS, IT MUST
BE MORE HUMAN, NOT LESS.

—Swift & Co., circa 1920

T   O   S   E   R   V   I   C   E

CARING IS EVERYTHING.

—Baron Friedrich Von Hugel

DEDICATION TO EXCELLENCE ON ANY
LEVEL, IN ANY AREA, REQUIRES AN
INTENSITY OF EMOTIONAL INVESTMENT.
UNFORTUNATELY, THERE ARE SCORES
OF PEOPLE WHO DO NOT MAKE THE
INVESTMENT—WHO DO NOT FEEL
STRONGLY ABOUT ANYTHING.

—Theodore Isaac Rubin

IF YOU CAN'T DO IT WITH FEELING, DON'T.

—Patsy Cline

40

C O M M I T M E N T

BEING A GOOD HUMAN IS GOOD BUSINESS.

—Paul Hawken

WHAT WE SAY AND WHAT WE DO
ULTIMATELY COMES BACK TO US SO LET US
OWN OUR RESPONSIBILITY, PLACE IT IN
OUR HANDS, AND CARRY IT WITH DIGNITY
AND STRENGTH.

—Gloria Evangelina Anzaldua

GOODNESS IS EASIER TO RECOGNIZE THAN
TO DEFINE.

—W.H. Auden

T O   S E R V I C E

WHILE TRYING TO THINK ABOUT HOW
YOU CAN MAKE A BIG DIFFERENCE,
TRY NOT TO IGNORE THE SMALL DAILY
DIFFERENCES YOU CAN MAKE.

—Marian Wright Edelman

I DO THE VERY BEST I KNOW HOW,
THE VERY BEST I CAN.

—Abraham Lincoln

WHAT YOU WILL DO MATTERS.   ALL YOU
NEED IS TO DO IT.

—Judy Grahn

C   O   M   M   I   T   M   E   N   T

NOTHING IS SO INFECTIOUS AS EXAMPLE.

—Charles Kingsley

PEOPLE MAY DOUBT WHAT WE SAY, BUT
THEY ALWAYS BELIEVE WHAT WE DO.

—Don Galer

NEVER ASK YOURSELF, "CAN I DO THIS?"
ASK INSTEAD, "HOW CAN I DO THIS?"

—Dan Zadra

TO SERVICE

THE MARK OF A TRUE PRO IS GIVING MORE
THAN YOU GET.

—Robert Kirby

IT IS THE SERVICE WE ARE NOT OBLIGED
TO GIVE THAT PEOPLE VALUE THE MOST.

—James C. Penney

GIVING PEOPLE A LITTLE MORE THAN
THEY EXPECT IS A GOOD WAY TO GET
BACK A LOT MORE THAN YOU'D EXPECT.

—Robert Half

COMMITMENT

BETTER THREE HOURS TOO SOON, THAN
ONE MINUTE TOO LATE.

—*William Shakespeare*

IT'S MORE IMPORTANT TO GO THE EXTRA
FOOT EVERY TIME THAN TO GO THE EXTRA
MILE NOW AND THEN.

—*Don Ward*

IN ALL MY YEARS IN SALES AND SERVICE
I HAVE NEVER ONCE HEARD A CUSTOMER
SAY, "JIM, THE THING I TREASURE
ABOUT OUR RELATIONSHIP IS THAT I
CAN 'ALMOST ALWAYS' COUNT ON YOU
TO BE THERE FOR ME."

—*Jim Williamson*

T O   S E R V I C E

WE CAN NEVER SEPARATE OUR BRAND
FROM OUR COMPANY.

—*Douglas Daft*

THE MOST IMPORTANT INGREDIENT WE
PUT INTO ANY RELATIONSHIP IS NOT
WHAT WE SAY OR WHAT WE DO, BUT
WHAT WE ARE.

—*Stephen Covey*

INTEGRITY IS WHAT WE DO, WHAT WE SAY,
AND WHAT WE SAY WE DO.

—*Don Galer*

C O M M I T M E N T

EVERY ACTION IS EITHER A CASE OF MAKING OR BREAKING A PROMISE. HAVING INTEGRITY MEANS ALWAYS KEEPING YOUR PROMISES TO YOURSELF OR OTHERS.

—Liz Guidera

IN A MOMENT OF DECISION, THE BEST THING YOU CAN DO IS THE RIGHT THING TO DO.

—Theodore Roosevelt

PURELY AND SIMPLY, WE MUST HAVE A DEEP COMMITMENT TO DO WHAT IS RIGHT, CONSISTENTLY, AND IN EVERY CIRCUMSTANCE —EVEN WHEN IT HURTS.

—Ken Baker

TO SERVICE

IT'S SIMPLE REALLY. JUST TRY TO PURSUE
EXCELLENCE WITH NO EXCUSES.

—Bill Campbell

NOT DOING MORE THAN AVERAGE IS
WHAT KEEPS THE AVERAGE DOWN.

—William Winans

THE DIFFERENCE BETWEEN GOOD AND
GREAT IS JUST THAT LITTLE EXTRA
EFFORT.

—Duffy Daugherty

COMMITMENT

ALL WHO HAVE MEANT GOOD WORK
WITH THEIR WHOLE HEART HAVE DONE
GOOD WORK.

—Robert Louis Stevenson

ATTITUDE IS A LITTLE THING THAT
MAKES A BIG DIFFERENCE.

—Mike Chestnut

WE WORK NOT ONLY TO PRODUCE BUT
TO GIVE VALUE TO TIME.

—Eugene Delacroix

T O   S E R V I C E

FROM NOW ON, ANY DEFINITION OF A
SUCCESSFUL LIFE MUST INCLUDE SERVING
OTHERS.

—George Bush

THINGS YOU DO FOR OTHER PEOPLE
ARE USUALLY SOME OF THE BEST THINGS
YOU DO.

—Gabriela Ortiz

I THINK I BEGAN LEARNING LONG AGO
THAT THOSE WHO ARE HAPPIEST ARE
THOSE WHO DO THE MOST FOR OTHERS.

—Booker T. Washington

50

C O M M I T M E N T

IT DOES NOT NEED TO BE A CHOICE BETWEEN HEAD DECISIONS AND HEART DECISIONS. AN ORGANIZATION THAT BALANCES HEAD DECISIONS AND HEART DECISIONS HAS A FAR GREATER POTENTIAL FOR ACHIEVING AND SUSTAINING SUCCESS THAN AN ORGANIZATION THAT DOESN'T HAVE HEART.

—Bill Maynard

IT'S TIME TO START THINKING WITH THE HEART.

—Beverley Wilson

THE REASON FOR DOING THINGS MUST
BE IMPORTANT ENOUGH TO EMPLOYEES
TO INFLUENCE THEIR CHOICES OF HOW
TO PERFORM WHEN THE BOSS IS NOT
WATCHING.

—Ferdinand F. Fournies

IT'S IMPOSSIBLE TO TREAT OUR
CUSTOMERS ANY BETTER THAN WE TREAT
OURSELVES.   GREAT SERVICE STARTS ON
THE INSIDE OF AN ORGANIZATION—WITH
THE WAY WE TREAT OUR CO-WORKERS
AND TEAMMATES—AND THEN WORKS ITS
WAY OUT.

—Dan Zadra

COMMITMENT

RULE #1: "USE YOUR GOOD JUDGMENT
IN ALL SITUATIONS." THERE WILL BE
NO ADDITIONAL RULES.

—Nordstrom Employee Manual

STATISTICS ARE NO SUBSTITUTE FOR
JUDGMENT.

—Henry Clay

A COMPANY'S CHARACTER IS KNOWN BY
THE PEOPLE IT KEEPS.

—John Ruskin

TO SERVICE

EVERYBODY CAN DO SOMETHING THAT
MAKES A DIFFERENCE.

—Todd R. Wagner

TO GIVE REAL SERVICE YOU MUST ADD
SOMETHING WHICH CANNOT BE BOUGHT
OR MEASURED WITH MONEY, AND THAT IS
SINCERITY AND INTEGRITY.

—Donald A. Adams

GOODWILL IS THE ONE AND ONLY ASSET
THAT COMPETITION CANNOT UNDERSELL
OR DESTROY.

—Marshall Field

COMMITMENT

TO YOUR CUSTOMER'S WAY OF THINKING,
YOU ARE THE COMPANY.

—*Ron Zemke*

TO MY CUSTOMER: I MAY NOT HAVE THE
ANSWER, BUT I'LL FIND IT. I MAY NOT
HAVE THE TIME, BUT I'LL MAKE TIME.
I MAY NOT BE THE BIGGEST, BUT I'LL BE
THE MOST COMMITTED TO YOUR SUCCESS.

—*Dan Zadra*

WOULD YOU DO BUSINESS WITH YOU?

—*Linda Silverman Goldzimer*

TO SERVICE

COMMITMENT TO

Teamwork has its own arithmetic. Combine two or more people in the pursuit of a common goal, and suddenly one-plus-one is more than two. Mutual trust

TEAMWORK

is an exponential power. Strengths are quickly multiplied, and problems swiftly divided. Together we are always able to accomplish what none of us could achieve alone.

UNITED WE STAND, DIVIDED WE FALL.

—Aesop

TEAMWORK IS BEING CONFIDENT THAT
YOU WILL HAVE THE PEOPLE, SUPPORT
AND RESOURCES BEHIND YOU WHEN YOU
REALLY NEED THEM. IT IS ALSO KNOWING
THAT YOU WILL BE READY AND ABLE TO
SUPPORT THOSE WHO RELY ON YOU.

—John Yanzek

TEAMWORK IS THE FUEL THAT ALLOWS
COMMON PEOPLE TO ATTAIN UNCOMMON
RESULTS.

—Fernando Bonaventura

COMMITMENT

TOGETHER WE ARE ALWAYS ABLE TO
ACCOMPLISH WHAT NONE OF US COULD
ACHIEVE ALONE.

—Dan Zadra

WHAT ONE CANNOT, ANOTHER CAN.

—William Davenant

THE WELFARE OF EACH IS BOUND UP
IN THE WELFARE OF ALL.

—Helen Keller

O   T E A M W O R K

ALONE WE CAN DO SO LITTLE, TOGETHER
WE CAN DO SO MUCH.

—Helen Keller

ANYTHING ONE PERSON CAN IMAGINE,
OTHER PEOPLE CAN MAKE REAL.

—Jules Verne

NO ONE CAN BE THE BEST AT EVERYTHING.
BUT WHEN ALL OF US COMBINE OUR
TALENTS, WE CAN BE THE BEST AT
VIRTUALLY ANYTHING.

—Dan Zadra

COMMITMENT

WE IS TERRIFIC.

—Unknown

RELATIONSHIPS CREATE THE FABRIC
OF OUR LIVES. THEY ARE THE FIBERS
THAT WEAVE ALL THINGS TOGETHER.

—Eden Froust

I'M GOOD; YOU'RE GOOD. TOGETHER
WE'RE BETTER.

—Dick Perl

NOTHING BINDS US ONE TO ANOTHER
LIKE A PROMISE KEPT.

—Mass Mutual

IF YOU WANT HELP, HELP OTHERS.
IF YOU WANT TRUST, TRUST OTHERS.
THAT'S HOW IT WORKS.

—Dan Zadra

TRUST EACH OTHER AGAIN AND AGAIN—
AND YOU WILL BUILD A GREAT TEAM.

—David Armistead

COMMITMENT

NOTHING IS PARTICULARLY HARD IF YOU
DIVIDE IT INTO SMALL JOBS.

—Henry Ford

IF EVERYONE SWEEPS IN FRONT OF THEIR
DOOR, THE WHOLE CITY WILL BE CLEAN.

—Urban proverb

A SYMPHONY MAY BE PLAYED BY A
HUNDRED MUSICIANS RESPONSIVE UNDER
THE BATON OF A MASTER CONDUCTOR, OR
BY FIFTY THOUSAND MECHANICS PLAYING
A BLUEPRINT SCORE.

—William J. Cameron

O   T   E   A   M   W   O   R   K

COMMITMENT IS WHAT MOVES A GROUP
TO BECOME A TEAM.

—David Quinlivan-Hall

MY WEAKNESS MAY BE YOUR STRENGTH,
AND VICE VERSA. WHEN WE WORK AS
A TEAM, THE STRENGTHS CANCEL THE
WEAKNESSES. THE RESULT IS MUTUAL
RESPECT THROUGHOUT THE ENTIRE TEAM.

—Mike Power

PULL TOGETHER AS ONE, LEARN FROM
EACH OTHER AND NEVER LET A
TEAMMATE FAIL.

—Rebecca Johnston

COMMITMENT

ORGANIZATIONS EXIST ONLY FOR ONE
PURPOSE: TO HELP PEOPLE REACH ENDS
TOGETHER THAT THEY COULDN'T ACHIEVE
INDIVIDUALLY.

—Robert H. Waterman

ONE STEP BY 100 PERSONS IS BETTER
THAN 100 STEPS BY ONE PERSON.

—Koichi Tsukamoto

THE WHOLE IS THE SUM OF ITS PARTS.
BE A GOOD PART.

—Nate McConnell

O   T   E   A   M   W   O   R   K

THE MASTERMIND PRINCIPLE: TWO OR
MORE PEOPLE ACTIVELY ENGAGED IN
PURSUIT OF A DEFINITE PURPOSE WITH A
POSITIVE MENTAL ATTITUDE, CONSTITUTE
AN UNBEATABLE FORCE.

—Napoleon Hill

VITAL TO EVERY WORTHWHILE OPERATION
IS COOPERATION.

—Frank Tyger

TAKE CARE OF THOSE WHO TAKE CARE
OF YOU.

—Tony Niccoli

C O M M I T M E N T

THE ORGANIZATION IS JUST THE VEHICLE
FOR HUMAN COOPERATION.

—Francis Gouillart

THE WORLD IS MOVED ALONG, NOT ONLY
BY THE MIGHTY SHOVES OF ITS HEROES,
BUT ALSO BY THE AGGREGATE OF THE
TINY PUSHES OF EACH HONEST WORKER.

—Helen Keller

THERE IS GREATNESS ALL AROUND YOU—
WELCOME IT! IT IS EASY TO BE GREAT
WHEN YOU GET AROUND GREAT PEOPLE.

—Bob Richards

O   T   E   A   M   W   O   R   K

THERE IS NO MORE NOBLE OCCUPATION
IN THE WORLD THAN TO ASSIST ANOTHER
HUMAN BEING—TO HELP SOMEONE
SUCCEED.

—Alan Loy McGinnis

WORKING TOGETHER WORKS!

—Dr. Rob Gilbert

ONCE WE ARE CONFIDENT OF OUR GOAL,
ALL WE NEED IS A LITTLE SUPPORT.

—Andre Laurendeau

COMMITMENT

MANY HANDS, HEARTS AND MINDS
GENERALLY CONTRIBUTE TO ANYONE'S
NOTABLE ACHIEVEMENTS.

—Walt Disney

NO MATTER WHAT YOU ACCOMPLISH IN
LIFE, SOMEBODY HELPS YOU.

—Wilma Rudolph

IF EVERYONE IS MOVING FORWARD
TOGETHER, THEN SUCCESS WILL TAKE
CARE OF ITSELF.

—Henry Ford

O   T E A M W O R K

EXCELLENCE IS NOT A SPECTATOR SPORT.
EVERYONE'S INVOLVED.

—Jack Welch

HELP PEOPLE REACH THEIR FULL
POTENTIAL: CATCH THEM DOING
SOMETHING RIGHT.

—Blanchard and Johnson

CELEBRATE WHAT YOU WANT
TO SEE MORE OF.

—Tom Peters

WE WON BECAUSE WE WERE ONE.

—Dr. Rob Gilbert

COMMITMENT

THERE ARE PLENTY OF TEAMS IN EVERY SPORT THAT HAVE GREAT PLAYERS AND NEVER WIN TITLES. MOST OF THE TIME, THOSE PLAYERS AREN'T WILLING TO SACRIFICE FOR THE GREATER GOOD OF THE TEAM. THE FUNNY THING IS, IN THE END, THEIR UNWILLINGNESS TO SACRIFICE ONLY MAKES INDIVIDUAL GOALS MORE DIFFICULT TO ACHIEVE. ONE THING I BELIEVE TO THE FULLEST IS THAT IF YOU THINK AND ACHIEVE AS A TEAM, THE INDIVIDUAL ACCOLADES WILL TAKE CARE OF THEMSELVES. TALENT WINS GAMES, BUT TEAMWORK AND INTELLIGENCE WIN CHAMPIONSHIPS.

—Michael Jordan

O T E A M W O R K

WHEN LARGE NUMBERS OF PEOPLE SHARE
THEIR JOY IN COMMON, THE HAPPINESS
OF EACH IS GREATER BECAUSE EACH ADDS
FUEL TO THE OTHER'S FLAME.

—Saint Augustine

IT IS A FUNDAMENTAL FACT OF LIFE THAT
YOU CAN SUCCEED BEST AND QUICKEST BY
HELPING OTHERS TO SUCCEED.

—Napoleon Hill

SOMETIMES OUR LIGHT GOES OUT BUT IS
BLOWN INTO FLAME BY ANOTHER HUMAN
BEING. EACH OF US OWES DEEPEST
THANKS TO THOSE WHO HAVE REKINDLED
THIS LIGHT.

—Albert Schweitzer

COMMITMENT

IF YOU HAVE KNOWLEDGE, LET OTHERS
LIGHT THEIR CANDLES AT IT.

—Margaret Fuller

GROUP DESIRE IS DIFFERENT THAN
INDIVIDUAL DESIRE. WITH INDIVIDUAL
DESIRE, IT'S UP TO YOU TO FEED THE
FIRE. WITH GROUP DESIRE, YOU GET ALL
KINDS OF PEOPLE ROLLING LOGS ON FROM
EVERY DIRECTION.

—Vince Pfaff

WE ARE CLOSEST TO PEOPLE WHEN WE HELP THEM GROW.

—*Milton Mayeroff*

HELP OTHERS BECOME WHAT THEY ARE CAPABLE OF BECOMING. BY CHOOSING TO THINK AND BELIEVE THE BEST ABOUT PEOPLE, YOU ARE ABLE TO BRING OUT THE BEST IN THEM.

—*Bob Moawad*

WE RISE BY LIFTING OTHERS.

—*Robert Green Ingersoll*

COMMITMENT

WE GAIN STRENGTH BY SHARING
STRENGTH.

—Don Ward

THERE IS NO SUCH THING AS A SELF-
MADE PERSON. WE REACH OUR GOALS
ONLY WITH THE HELP OF OTHERS.

—George Shinn

THOSE WHOM WE SUPPORT HOLD US
UP IN LIFE.

—Marie Ebner von Eshenbach

O   T   E   A   M   W   O   R   K

THERE IS SOMEBODY SMARTER THAN
ANY OF US, AND THAT IS ALL OF US.

—Michael Nolan

PROGRESS IS NINETY-FIVE PERCENT
ROUTINE TEAMWORK. THE OTHER
FIVE PERCENT RELIES ON NEW
AND BETTER IDEAS.

—Michael LeBoeuf

PEOPLE RESIST THAT WHICH IS FORCED
UPON THEM. PEOPLE SUPPORT THAT
WHICH THEY HELP TO CREATE.

—Vince Pfaff

C O M M I T M E N T

NO ONE WANTS ADVICE, WE WANT
COLLABORATION.

—Rian Jones

MOTIVATION IS EVERYTHING. YOU HAVE
TO INSPIRE THE NEXT GUY DOWN THE LINE
AND GET HIM TO INSPIRE HIS PEOPLE.

77

—Lee Iacocca

HELP OTHERS GET AHEAD. YOU ALWAYS
STAND TALLER WITH SOMEONE ELSE ON
YOUR SHOULDERS.

—Bob Moawad

O   T E A M W O R K

WE MUST REMEMBER THAT ONE
DETERMINED PERSON CAN MAKE A
SIGNIFICANT DIFFERENCE, AND THAT
A SMALL GROUP OF DETERMINED PEOPLE
CAN CHANGE THE COURSE OF HISTORY.

—Sonia Johnson

EACH OF US HAS SPECIAL TALENTS. IT'S
OUR DUTY TO MAKE THE MOST OF THEM.

—Robert E. Allen

EACH PERSON GROWS NOT ONLY BY HER
OWN TALENTS AND DEVELOPMENT OF
HER INNER BELIEFS, BUT ALSO BY WHAT
SHE RECEIVES FROM THE PEOPLE
AROUND HER.

—Iris Haberli

C O M M I T M E N T

IT TAKES EACH OF US TO MAKE A
DIFFERENCE FOR ALL OF US.

—Jackie Mutcheson

WORKING TOGETHER, ORDINARY PEOPLE
CAN PERFORM EXTRAORDINARY FEATS.
THEY CAN PUSH THINGS THAT COME
INTO THEIR HANDS A LITTLE HIGHER
UP, A LITTLE FARTHER ON TOWARDS
THE HEIGHTS OF EXCELLENCE.

—B.J. Marshall

O   O   T   E   A   M   W   O   R   K

COMMITMENT TO

Imagination is our most precious power. The best way to predict the future is to invent it. We aren't stuck with the present; at any moment we are free to create an exciting new

INNOVATION

reality. Just form a picture in your mind's eye. Think of something that would be wonderful if it were only possible. Then go back and do whatever it takes to make it real.

IT IS THE IMAGINATION THAT GIVES
SHAPE TO THE UNIVERSE.

—Barry Lopez

THE HISTORY OF HUMANITY IS THE
HISTORY OF IDEAS.

—Ludwig von Mises

EXCELLENT ORGANIZATIONS AND TEAMS
ARE EXPERIMENTERS SUPREME.

—Tom Peters

COMMITMENT

EVERY GREAT ADVANCE HAS
ISSUED FROM A NEW AUDACITY OF
IMAGINATION.

—John Dewey

THE IMPOSSIBLE IS OFTEN THE
UNTRIED.

—Jim Goodwin

THE HUMAN MIND, ONCE STRETCHED
BY A NEW IDEA, NEVER REGAINS ITS
ORIGINAL DIMENSIONS.

—Oliver Wendell Holmes

INNOVATION

YESTERDAY'S ANSWER USUALLY HAS
NOTHING TO DO WITH TODAY'S PROBLEM.

—Bill Gates

YOU CAN'T SOLVE A PROBLEM ON THE
SAME LEVEL THAT IT WAS CREATED.
YOU HAVE TO RISE ABOVE IT TO THE
NEXT LEVEL.

—Albert Einstein

IF WE WOULD HAVE NEW KNOWLEDGE,
WE MUST GET A WHOLE NEW WORLD OF
QUESTIONS.

—Susan K. Langer

COMMITMENT

WE KEEP MOVING FORWARD, OPENING NEW
DOORS, AND DOING NEW THINGS, BECAUSE
WE'RE CURIOUS AND CURIOSITY KEEPS
LEADING US DOWN NEW PATHS.

—Walt Disney

YOU DON'T UNDERSTAND ANYTHING UNTIL
YOU LEARN IT MORE THAN ONE WAY.

—Marvin Minsky

DISCOVERIES ARE OFTEN MADE BY NOT
FOLLOWING INSTRUCTIONS, BY GOING OFF
THE MAIN ROAD, BY TRYING THE UNTRIED.

—Frank Tyger

INNOVATION

VISION REACHES BEYOND THE THING
THAT IS, INTO THE CONCEPTION OF
WHAT CAN BE. IMAGINATION GIVES
YOU THE PICTURE. VISION GIVES YOU
THE IMPULSE TO MAKE THE PICTURE
YOUR OWN.

—Robert Collier

INSPIRATION AND IMAGINATION GO
HAND IN HAND.

—Susan Fielder

DON'T BE CONFINED BY REALITY. THINK
ABOUT WHAT COULD BE ACCOMPLISHED
IF THERE WERE NO BOUNDARIES.

—James Fantus

COMMITMENT

ALL ACTS PERFORMED IN THE WORLD
BEGIN IN THE IMAGINATION.

—Barbara Grizzuti Harrison

BEFORE YOU GET YOUR QUESTIONS
ANSWERED YOU HAVE TO GET THEM
ASKED.

—Bill Farr

YOU CAN'T COUNT ON CONVENTIONAL
WISDOM ANYMORE.

—Bill Gates

INNOVATION

TO IMPROVE IS TO CHANGE. TO BE
PERFECT IS TO CHANGE OFTEN.

—Winston Churchill

ONE'S WORK MAY BE FINISHED SOMEDAY,
BUT ONE'S EDUCATION NEVER.

—Alexandre Dumas

ALWAYS BE A "WORK IN PROGRESS."

—Emily Lillan

COMMITMENT

EVERY DAY LEARN SOMETHING NEW.

—Holly Solomon

THERE IS NO SUCH THING AS AN
INSIGNIFICANT IMPROVEMENT.

—Tom Peters

THERE IS A WAY TO DO IT BETTER—
FIND IT.

—Thomas Edison

INNOVATION

IF IT AIN'T BROKE, FIX IT. TAKE FAST.
MAKE IT FASTER. TAKE SMART. MAKE IT
BRILLIANT. TAKE GOOD. MAKE IT GREAT.

—*CIGNA Advertisement*

IF WE ALWAYS DO WHAT WE ALWAYS
DID, WE WILL ALWAYS GET WHAT WE
ALWAYS GOT.

—*Jackie "Moms" Mabley*

THE INNOVATOR IS NOT AN OPPONENT OF
THE OLD, HE IS A PROPONENT OF
THE NEW.

—*Lyle E. Shaller*

C O M M I T M E N T

THE GREAT LEADERS DON'T RESIST
INNOVATION, THEY SYMBOLIZE IT.

—David Ogilvy

I THINK LEADERS SHOULD ENCOURAGE
THE NEXT GENERATION NOT JUST TO
FOLLOW, BUT TO OVERTAKE.

—Anita Roddick

THE NEXT GENERATION WILL UNDER-
STAND YOU. THE REAL CHALLENGE IS TO
CONVINCE YOUR PEERS TODAY.

—Camille Pisarro

I N N O V A T I O N

ALWAYS BE ON THE LOOKOUT FOR THE
BIG IDEA THAT CAN CHANGE YOUR LIFE
AND THE LIVES OF OTHERS.

—Norman Vincent Peale

IDEAS ARE ALL AROUND US, BUT WE MUST
BE OBSERVANT SO WE CAN CATCH THEM
WHIZZING BY.

—Marlene Caroselli

GREAT ACCOMPLISHMENTS HAVE
ALWAYS RESULTED, NOT MERELY FROM
THE TRANSMISSION OF IDEAS, BUT
ENTHUSIASM.

—Anonymous

COMMITMENT

ONCE A NEW IDEA SPRINGS INTO
EXISTENCE, IT CANNOT BE UNTHOUGHT.
THERE IS A SENSE OF IMMORTALITY IN
A NEW IDEA.

—Edward De Bono

IDEAS COME FROM EVERYWHERE.

—Alfred Hitchcock

TRUST YOUR CRAZY IDEAS.

—Dan Zadra

INNOVATION

CREATIVITY COMES FROM TRUST.
TRUST YOUR INSTINCTS.

—Rita Mae Brown

THE WORLD OF REALITY HAS ITS
LIMITS; THE WORLD OF IMAGINATION
IS BOUNDLESS.

—Jean-Jacques Rousseau

THE FUTURE IS UNCERTAIN...BUT THIS
UNCERTAINTY IS AT THE VERY HEART
OF HUMAN CREATIVITY.

—Ilya Prigogine, Nobel Chemist

COMMITMENT

CREATIVITY IS THE MOST EFFECTIVE
RESPONSE TO RAPID CHANGE, AND ALL
BREAKTHROUGHS RELY HEAVILY ON
CREATIVITY.

—Robert Porter Lynch

CREATIVITY IS INVENTING, EXPERI-
MENTING, GROWING, TAKING RISKS,
BREAKING RULES, MAKING MISTAKES,
AND HAVING FUN.

—Mary L. Cook

CREATIVITY CAN SOLVE ALMOST ANY
PROBLEM. THE CREATIVE ACT, THE
DEFEAT OF HABIT BY ORIGINALITY,
OVERCOMES EVERYTHING.

—Goerge Lois

INNOVATION

IT ISN'T THAT THEY CAN'T SEE THE
SOLUTION. IT IS THAT THEY CAN'T SEE
THE PROBLEM.

—G.K. Chesterton

A GOOD PROBLEM WILL GATHER YOU UP
AT YOUR TENDER, GROWING EDGE AND
CHANGE WHO YOU ARE.

—Robert Kegan

FAILURE IS A NORMAL, NATURAL WAY OF
MAPPING THE UNKNOWN.

—Jack Matson

COMMITMENT

JUST BECAUSE SOMETHING DOESN'T DO
WHAT YOU PLANNED IT TO DO DOESN'T
MEAN IT'S USELESS.

—Thomas Edison

MY ERRORS WERE MORE FERTILE THAN
I EVER IMAGINED.

—Jan Tschichold

EACH PROBLEM THAT I SOLVED BECAME
A RULE WHICH SERVED AFTERWARDS TO
SOLVE OTHER PROBLEMS.

—Rene Descartes

INNOVATION

AN INVASION OF ARMIES CAN BE
RESISTED, BUT NOT AN IDEA WHOSE
TIME HAS COME.

—Victor Hugo

ALL GREAT IDEAS ARE CONTROVERSIAL,
OR HAVE BEEN AT ONE TIME.

—George Seldes

A ROCK PILE CEASES TO BE A ROCK
PILE THE MOMENT A SINGLE MAN
CONTEMPLATES IT, BEARING WITHIN
HIM THE IMAGE OF A CATHEDRAL.

—Antoine de Saint-Exupery

COMMITMENT

THE PRINCIPAL MARK OF GENIUS IS NOT
PERFECTION BUT ORIGINALITY, THE
OPENING OF NEW FRONTIERS.

—Arthur Koestler

IT'S BETTER TO HAVE THE PHILOSOPHY
TO OUT-THINK YOUR COMPETITION THAN
OUTSPEND THEM.

—Les Wolff

IMITATORS COPY AN IDEA; INNOVATORS
BUILD ON IT.

—Dan Zadra

I N N O V A T I O N

TO KNOW IS NOTHING AT ALL;
TO IMAGINE IS EVERYTHING.

—*Anatole France*

IMAGINATION IS THE BEGINNING OF
CREATION. WE IMAGINE WHAT WE DESIRE,
WE WILL WHAT WE IMAGINE; AND AT LAST
WE CREATE WHAT WE WILL.

—*George Bernard Shaw*

MEASURE YOURSELF BY THE STRETCH
OF YOUR IMAGINATION.

—*Robert Schuller*

COMMITMENT

**CHANGE STARTS WHEN SOMEONE
SEES THE NEXT STEP.**

—William Drayton

**YOU MUST BE READY NOT ONLY TO
TAKE THE OPPORTUNITIES, BUT TO
MAKE THEM.**

—Kobi Yamada

**WHAT IS CENTRAL TO BUSINESS IS
THE JOY OF CREATING.**

—Peter Robinson

INNOVATION

HOWEVER GRADUAL THE COURSE OF
HISTORY, THERE MUST ALWAYS BE THE
DAY, EVEN AN HOUR AND MINUTE, WHEN
SOME SIGNIFICANT ACTION IS PERFORMED
FOR THE FIRST OR LAST TIME.

—Peter Quennell

INNOVATION COMES ONLY FROM READILY
AND SEAMLESSLY SHARING INFORMATION
RATHER THAN HOARDING IT.

—Tom Peters

CONTINUOUS IMPROVEMENT STARVES
WITHOUT CONTINUOUS COMMUNICATION.

—Dan Zadra

C O M M I T M E N T

IF YOUR EXPERIENCES WOULD BENEFIT
ANYBODY, GIVE THEM TO SOMEONE.

—Florence Nightingale

WE HAVE TO TEACH AS WELL AS LEARN.

—Gloria Steinem

WE'RE ALL WORKING TOGETHER;
THAT'S THE SECRET.

—Sam Walton

INNOVATION

COMMITMENT TO

Aim high in work and life.

Become the very best you

that you were meant to

be. Defy discouragement,

stay true to your dreams.

Look the world straight in

the eye. Make a difference

S U C C E S S

in the lives of others.

Laugh often and love much.

Above all, celebrate every

step of the way—not just

the great achievements but

the great attempts.

NO ONE RISES TO LOW EXPECTATIONS.

—Les Brown

YOU CAN'T HIT A TARGET YOU CANNOT
SEE, AND YOU CANNOT SEE A TARGET
YOU DO NOT HAVE.

—Zig Ziglar

NEVER TURN DOWN AN OPPORTUNITY
BECAUSE YOU THINK IT'S TOO SMALL;
YOU DON'T KNOW WHERE IT CAN LEAD.

—Julia Morgan

COMMITMENT

WHAT YOU GET BY ACHIEVING YOUR GOALS
IS NOT AS IMPORTANT AS WHAT YOU
BECOME BY ACHIEVING YOUR GOALS.

—Zig Ziglar

THE SECRETS OF MAKING DREAMS COME
TRUE CAN BE SUMMARIZED IN FOUR C'S.
THEY ARE CURIOSITY, CONFIDENCE,
COURAGE, AND CONSTANCY, AND THE
GREATEST OF ALL IS CONFIDENCE.
WHEN YOU BELIEVE IN A THING, BELIEVE
IN IT ALL THE WAY, IMPLICITLY AND
UNQUESTIONABLY.

—Walt Disney

DREAMS AND DEDICATION ARE A
POWERFUL COMBINATION FOR GOOD.

—William Longgood

T O   S U C C E S S

SUCCESS DEPENDS ON WHERE
INTENTION IS.

—*Gita Bellin*

THE SECRET TO JOY IN WORK IS
CONTAINED IN ONE WORD—EXCELLENCE.
TO KNOW HOW TO DO SOMETHING WELL
IS TO ENJOY IT.

—*Pearl S. Buck*

YOUR WORK IS TO DISCOVER YOUR WORK
AND THEN WITH ALL YOUR HEART TO GIVE
YOURSELF TO IT.

—*Buddha*

COMMITMENT

YOU HAVE TO HAVE YOUR HEART IN THE
BUSINESS, AND THE BUSINESS IN YOUR
HEART.

—Thomas J. Watson, Sr.

WE RARELY SUCCEED AT ANYTHING
UNLESS WE HAVE FUN DOING IT.

—Rev. John Naus

PEOPLE WHO FEEL GOOD ABOUT
THEMSELVES PRODUCE GOOD RESULTS.

—Ken Blanchard

T   O   S   U   C   C   E   S   S

IT'S YOUR LIFE, YOUR ONE AND ONLY
LIFE—SO TAKE EXCELLENCE VERY
PERSONALLY.

—Scott Johnson

WE DO NOT BELIEVE IF WE DO NOT LIVE
AND WORK ACCORDING TO OUR BELIEF.

—Heidi Wills

EXCELLENT THINGS ARE RARE.

—Plato

COMMITMENT

COMMIT TO YOUR JOB AND YOUR WORK,
WHATEVER IT IS. BELIEVE IN IT MORE
THAN ANYTHING ELSE. IF YOU LOVE YOUR
WORK, YOU'LL BE OUT THERE EVERY DAY
TRYING TO DO THE BEST YOU CAN, AND
PRETTY SOON EVERYBODY AROUND WILL
CATCH THE PASSION FROM YOU.

—Sam Walton

IF YOU WANT TO ACHIEVE EXCELLENCE,
YOU CAN GET THERE TODAY. AS OF
THIS SECOND, QUIT DOING LESS THAN
EXCELLENT WORK.

—Thomas J. Watson, Sr.

T   O   S   U   C   C   E   S   S

AD ASTRA PER ASPERA. (TO THE STARS
THROUGH HARDSHIP.)

—Motto of the State of Kansas

I BELIEVE IN LUCK AS MUCH AS THE
NEXT PERSON—I'M JUST NOT GOING TO
WAIT FOR IT.

—Kobi Yamada

IF YOU ARE PREPARED, YOU HAVE
THE EDGE. IF YOU HAVE THE EDGE,
YOU SUCCEED.

—Unknown

COMMITMENT

NEVER MISTAKE ACTIVITY FOR
ACHIEVEMENT.

—Mabel Newcomber

REAL EXCELLENCE DOES NOT COME
CHEAPLY. A CERTAIN PRICE MUST BE
PAID IN TERMS OF PRACTICE, PATIENCE,
AND PERSISTENCE—NATURAL ABILITY
NOTWITHSTANDING.

—Stephen Covey

IT TAKES A LONG TIME TO BRING
EXCELLENCE TO MATURITY.

—Publius Syrus

TO SUCCESS

SOME SUCCEED BECAUSE THEY ARE
DESTINED TO; MOST SUCCEED BECAUSE
THEY ARE DETERMINED TO.

—Anatole France

ONE OF LIFE'S MOST PAINFUL MOMENTS
COMES WHEN WE MUST ADMIT THAT WE
DIDN'T DO OUR HOMEWORK, THAT WE
ARE NOT PREPARED.

—Merlin Olsen

THERE'S A BIG DIFFERENCE BETWEEN
SEEING AN OPPORTUNITY AND SEIZING
AN OPPORTUNITY.

—Jim Moore

C O M M I T M E N T

WORK WILL ALWAYS WIN WHAT WISHING WON'T.

—Michael Nolan

ONE OF THE MOST DIFFICULT THINGS EVERYONE HAS TO LEARN IS THAT FOR YOUR ENTIRE LIFE YOU MUST KEEP FIGHTING AND ADJUSTING IF YOU HOPE TO SURVIVE. NO MATTER WHO YOU ARE OR WHAT YOUR POSITION YOU MUST KEEP FIGHTING FOR WHATEVER IT IS YOU DESIRE TO ACHIEVE.

—George Allen

SUCCESS CAN ONLY BE MEASURED IN TERMS OF DISTANCE TRAVELED.

—Mavis Gallant

T O   S U C C E S S

FAILURE IS NOT AN OPTION.

—Brett Mullen

**SHOW ME SOMEONE WHO HAS DONE
SOMETHING WORTHWHILE, AND I'LL
SHOW YOU SOMEONE WHO HAS OVERCOME
ADVERSITY.**

—Lou Holtz

**NO ONE WOULD EVER HAVE CROSSED THE
OCEAN IF HE OR SHE COULD HAVE GOTTEN
OFF THE SHIP IN A STORM.**

—Charles Kettering

COMMITMENT

DIFFICULTY IS THE EXCUSE HISTORY
NEVER ACCEPTS.

—Edward R. Murrow

WE CAN NO LONGER WAIT FOR THE
STORM TO PASS. WE MUST LEARN TO
WORK IN THE RAIN.

—Peter Silas

THE WORLD STANDS ASIDE TO LET
ANYONE PASS WHO KNOWS WHERE HE
IS GOING.

—David Starr Jordan

TO SUCCESS

THE LADDER OF ACHIEVEMENT DOESN'T CARE WHO CLIMBS IT.

—Dr. Rob Gilbert

I AM NOT BOUND TO WIN, BUT I AM BOUND TO BE TRUE. I AM NOT BOUND TO SUCCEED, BUT I AM BOUND TO LIVE UP TO WHAT LIGHT I MIGHT HAVE.

—Abraham Lincoln

DECIDE TO BE YOUR BEST. IN THE LONG RUN THE WORLD IS GOING TO WANT AND HAVE THE BEST, AND THAT MIGHT AS WELL BE YOU.

—Booker T. Washington

COMMITMENT

THE SECRET OF SUCCESS IS CONSTANCY
OF PURPOSE.

—Benjamin Disraeli

FIND A PURPOSE IN LIFE SO BIG IT
WILL CHALLENGE EVERY CAPACITY TO
BE AT YOUR BEST.

—Jim Loehr

I DIDN'T COME HERE TO BE AVERAGE.

—Michael Jordan

T   O   S   U   C   C   E   S   S

ONE BY ONE, WE CAN BE THE BETTER
WORLD WE WISH FOR.

—*Kobi Yamada*

IMAGINE WHAT WILL HAPPEN IF EACH
OF US DECIDES TO REACH JUST A LITTLE
BIT HIGHER, TO TRY JUST A LITTLE BIT
HARDER, TO CARE JUST A LITTLE BIT
MORE.   THAT'S THE POWER OF ONE.
YOU'VE GOT THAT POWER—USE IT!

—*Ron Kendrick*

IT IS UP TO EACH OF US TO MAKE THE
BEST USE OF OUR TIME TO HELP CREATE
A BETTER WORLD.

—*Dalai Lama*

C O M M I T M E N T

NOT TO GO OUT AND DO YOUR BEST
IS TO SACRIFICE THE GIFT.

—Steve Prefontaine

SUCCESS IN LIFE HAS NOTHING TO
DO WITH WHAT YOU GAIN IN LIFE OR
ACCOMPLISH FOR YOURSELF. IT'S WHAT
YOU DO FOR OTHERS.

—Danny Thomas

HEART, INSTINCT, PRINCIPLES.

—Blaise Pascal

I USE THE BUSINESS TO MAKE GREAT
PEOPLE. I DON'T USE PEOPLE TO MAKE
A GREAT BUSINESS.

—Ralph Stayer

THERE ARE ONLY TWO GUIDELINES:
WHAT'S IN THE LONG-TERM BEST
INTERESTS OF THE ENTERPRISE AND
ITS STAKEHOLDERS, SUPPLEMENTED
BY THE DOMINANT CONCERN OF DOING
WHAT'S RIGHT.

—Robert D. Haas

IT IS MORE IMPORTANT TO DO THE RIGHT
THINGS THAN TO DO THINGS RIGHT.

—Peter Drucker

COMMITMENT

THINGS WHICH MATTER MOST MUST
NEVER BE AT THE MERCY OF THINGS
WHICH MATTER LEAST.

—Johann Von Goethe

TOMORROW, WHO WILL REALLY CARE
HOW FAST WE GREW? ISN'T IT MORE
IMPORTANT TO KNOW WHAT WE ARE
BUILDING WITH OUR GROWTH, AND WHY?
MEASURING MORE IS EASY; MEASURING
BETTER IS HARD. MEASURING BETTER
REQUIRES A CLEAR MISSION, AN EXCITING
VISION AND SHARED VALUES.

—Ron Kendrick

TO SUCCESS

NO ONE EVER ATTAINS EMINENT
SUCCESS BY SIMPLY DOING WHAT IS
REQUIRED; IT IS THE AMOUNT AND
EXCELLENCE OF WHAT IS OVER AND
ABOVE THE REQUIRED THAT DETERMINES
THE ULTIMATE DISTINCTION.

—*Charles Kendall Adams*

THE HEIGHT OF YOUR ACCOMPLISHMENT
WILL EQUAL THE DEPTH OF YOUR
CONVICTIONS.

—*William F. Scolavino*

COMMITMENT

DO YOU WANT TO BE SAFE AND GOOD,
OR DO YOU WANT TO TAKE A CHANCE
AND BE GREAT?

—Jimmy Johnson

SOMETIMES YOU JUST HAVE TO CREATE
WHAT YOU WANT TO BE A PART OF.

—Geri Weitzman

THE MORE WE DO, THE MORE WE CAN DO.

—William Hazlitt

TO SUCCESS

BEGIN WITH LIFE AS YOU FIND IT AND
MAKE IT BETTER.

—Carter G. Woodson

ONE LIFE STAMPS AND INFLUENCES
ANOTHER, WHICH IN TURN STAMPS
AND INFLUENCES ANOTHER, ON AND ON
UNTIL THE SOUL OF HUMAN EXPERIENCE
BREATHES ON IN GENERATIONS WE'LL
NEVER EVEN MEET.

—Mary Kay Blakely

THE QUALITY OF A PERSON'S LIFE IS IN
DIRECT PROPORTION TO HIS COMMITMENT
TO EXCELLENCE.

—Vince Lombardi

COMMITMENT

SUCCESS NEVER RESTS. ON YOUR WORST
DAYS, BE GOOD. AND ON YOUR BEST DAYS,
BE GREAT. AND ON EVERY OTHER DAY,
GET BETTER.

—Carmen Mariano

DESIRE IS THE KEY TO MOTIVATION,
BUT IT'S THE DETERMINATION AND
COMMITMENT TO AN UNRELENTING
PURSUIT OF OUR GOAL—A COMMITMENT
TO EXCELLENCE—THAT WILL ENABLE US TO
ATTAIN THE SUCCESS WE SEEK.

—Mario Andretti

T O   S U C C E S S

Also available from Compendium Publishing are these spirited
and compelling companion books of great quotations.

BE HAPPY.
Remember to Live, Love,
Laugh and Learn

BECAUSE OF YOU™
Celebrating the Difference You Make™

BRILLIANCE™
Uncommon Voices From
Uncommon Women™

EVERYONE LEADS™
It takes each of us to make
a difference for all of us

FOREVER REMEMBERED™
A Gift for the Grieving Heart.

I BELIEVE IN YOU™
To your heart, your dream and
the difference you make

LITTLE MIRACLES™
To renew your dreams, lift your
spirits, and strengthen your resolve

REACH FOR THE STARS™
Give up the Good to Go for the Great

THANK YOU
In appreciation of you,
and all that you do

TOGETHER WE CAN™
Celebrating the power of
a team and a dream™

TO YOUR SUCCESS™
Thoughts to Give Wings to Your
Work and Your Dreams™

WHATEVER IT TAKES™
A Journey into the Heart
of Human Achievement™

YOU'VE GOT A FRIEND™
Thoughts to Celebrate
the Joy of Friendship™

These books may be ordered directly from the publisher (800) 914-3327.
But please try your bookstore first!

www.compendiuminc.com